MENTAL PEACE And EMOTIONAL HEALING Through God's Word

TABLE OF CONTENTS

CHAPTER ONE

WHAT TO DO WHEN DEPRESSION AND WORRY COME KNOCKING

Depression and worry are some of the mental illnesses no one deserves to go through. They hinder your life in more ways than one. A lot of people go through depression with no hope in sight. They don't see any reason to keep on living.

Depression stunts your personal growth, cripples your progress and confuses your thoughts. It keeps you from everything good and useful while wreaking havoc on your soul. Even the activity you once enjoyed becomes boring, lifeless and unfulfilling.

You cannot fight all your battles in your own strength. You can't hate yourself forever. You cannot afford to weep alone, to lock yourself up as though you have come to the end of the road. Doing that will increase the symptoms, multiply and nightmares, and make it harder to overcome your mental trouble.

God loves you and doesn't want you to keep like that anymore. He has a plan for you, a way to get back up and move on with what is left of your life. In fact, God is giving you a new life. Through His word, you can kick depression, worry and anxiety out of your life. These enemies of happiness are no longer allowed in your life. It is time to kick them out once and for all.

Hand over everything to God.

There is no emotion bigger than God or stronger than the word of God.

God's word contains facts about who you are and what you can do.

The Bible speaks about you, not about Moses, Abraham and Peter.

Make personal application of God's word every time you read or study it.

Here are a few scripture that speaks on depression and worry:

"BE anxious for nothing, but in everything by prayer and supplication, with thanksgiving, let your requests be made known to God; and the peace of God, which surpasses all understanding, will guard your hearts and minds through Christ Jesus." Philippians 4:6-7.

"Fear not, for I am with you; Be not dismayed, for I am your God. I will strengthen you, Yes, I will help you, I will uphold you with My righteous right hand" Isaiah 41:10.

"Therefore I say to you, do not worry about your life, what you will eat or what you will drink; nor about your body, what you will put on. Is not life more than food and the body more than clothing?" Matthew 6:25.

"Casting all your care upon Him, for He cares for you" 1 Peter 5:7. "Therefore do not worry about tomorrow, for tomorrow will worry about its own things. Sufficient for the day is its own trouble" Matthew 6:34.

"In the multitude of my anxieties within me, Your comforts delight my soul" Psalm 94:19.

"Let not your heart be troubled; you believe in God, believe also in Me" John 14:1.

"Peace I leave with you, My peace I give to you; not as the world gives do I give to you. Let not your heart be troubled, neither let it be afraid" John 14:27.

“Anxiety in the heart of man causes depression, But a good word makes it glad” Proverbs 12:25.

“Lord, all my desire is before You; And my sighing is not hidden from You” Psalm 38:9.

“For in much wisdom is much grief, And he who increases knowledge increases sorrow” Ecclesiastes 1:18.

“Do not worry about your life, what you will eat; nor about the body, what you will put on. Life is more than food, and the body is more than clothing" Luke 12:22b-23.

"And God is able to make all grace abound toward you, that you, always having all sufficiency in all things, may have an abundance for every good work" 2 Corinthians 9:8.

"Therefore remove sorrow from your heart, And put away evil from your flesh, For childhood and youth are vanity" Ecclesiastes 11:10.

"But when they arrest you and deliver you up, do not worry beforehand, or premeditate what you will speak. But whatever is given you in that hour, speak that; for it is not you who speak, but the Holy Spirit" Mark 13:11.

"Now he who received seed among the thorns is he who hears the word, and the cares of this world and the deceitfulness of riches choke the word, and he becomes unfruitful" Matthew 13:22.

"And I heard a loud voice from heaven saying, "Behold, the tabernacle of God is with men, and He will dwell with them, and they shall be His people.

God Himself will be with them and be their God. And God will wipe away every tear from their eyes; there shall be no more death, nor sorrow, nor crying. There shall be no more pain, for the former things have passed away" Revelation 21:3-4.

"Then Job arose, tore his robe, and shaved his head; and he fell to the ground and worshiped. And he said: "Naked I came from my mother's womb, And naked shall I return there. The Lord gave, and the Lord has taken away; Blessed be the name of the Lord" Job 1:20-21.

"Consider the ravens, for they neither sow nor reap, which have neither storehouse nor barn; and God feeds them. Of how much more value are you than the birds?" Luke 12:24.

"For I know that my Redeemer lives, And He shall stand at last on the earth" Job 19:25.

"The righteous cry out, and the Lord hears, And delivers them out of all their troubles. The Lord is near to those who have a broken heart, And saves such as have a contrite spirit" Psalm 34:17-18.

“And the Lord, He is the One who goes before you. He will be with you, He will not leave you nor forsake you; do not fear nor be dismayed”
Deuteronomy 31:8.

“Blessed are those who mourn, For they shall be comforted”
Matthew 5:4.

“Casting all your care upon Him, for He cares for you” 1 Peter 5:7.

“For His anger is but for a moment, His favor is for life; Weeping may endure for a night, But joy comes in the morning” Psalm 30:5.

“For in much wisdom is much grief, And he who increases knowledge increases sorrow” Ecclesiastes 1:18.

“Lord, all my desire is before You; And my sighing is not hidden from You” Psalm 38:9.

“And I heard a loud voice from heaven saying, “Behold, the tabernacle of God is with men, and He will dwell with them, and they shall be His people. God Himself will be with them and be their God. And God will wipe away every tear from their eyes; there shall be no more death, nor sorrow, nor crying. There shall be no more pain, for the former things have passed away" Revelation 21:3-4.

"Therefore remove sorrow from your heart, And put away evil from your flesh, For childhood and youth are vanity" Ecclesiastes 11:10.

"As sorrowful, yet always rejoicing; as poor, yet making many rich; as having nothing, and yet possessing all things" 2 Corinthians 6:10.

"Rejoice with those who rejoice, and weep with those who weep" Romans 12:15.

"They shall neither hunger anymore nor thirst anymore; the sun shall not strike them, nor any heat; for the Lamb who is in the midst of the throne will shepherd them and lead them to living fountains of waters. And God will wipe away every tear from their eyes" Revelation 7:16-17.

"Now, therefore," says the Lord, "Turn to Me with all your heart, With fasting, with weeping, and with mourning" Joel 2:12.

“Then Job arose, tore his robe, and shaved his head; and he fell to the ground and worshiped. And he said: “Naked I came from my mother’s womb, And naked shall I return there. The Lord gave, and the Lord has taken away; Blessed be the name of the Lord” Job 1:20-21”

“Return and tell Hezekiah the leader of My people, ‘Thus says the Lord, the God of David your father: “I have heard your prayer, I have seen your tears; surely I will heal you. On the third day you shall go up to the house of the Lord"' 2 Kings 20:5.

"A wise son makes a glad father, But a foolish son is the grief of his mother" Proverbs 10:1.

"The vine has dried up, And the fig tree has withered; The pomegranate tree, The palm tree also, And the apple tree— All the trees of the field are withered; Surely joy has withered away from the sons of men" Joel 1:12.

"The Lord opens the eyes of the blind; The Lord raises those who are bowed down; The Lord loves the righteous" Psalm 146:8.

"And do not grieve the Holy Spirit of God, by whom you were sealed for the day of redemption" Ephesians 4:30.

"Hear my prayer, O Lord, And give ear to my cry; Do not be silent at my tears; For I am a stranger with You, A sojourner, as all my fathers were" Psalm 39:12.

CHAPTER TWO

LETTER FROM GOD

Nothing works so amazingly like a timely word of encouragement from someone who knows what you are going through in life. Sometimes, starting afresh is painful and scary. But you it may be all you need to do to move forward. Yet trying to make your life better can take its toll on you. But with the right encouragement, you will discover that you are stronger than you feel and tougher than you think.

God knows you better than anyone else He sees all and has power over visible and invisible things. He understands your situation better than you do and His word can guide you along the way. Trust God and take His words of encouragement for what it is. Allow it to produce in you the courage to forget the past or your present negative feelings. Receive the power to move on with your life.

You must never forget that God loves you always.

True courage is found in a fearful heart.

When you are fed up with life, always remember that all hope is not lost yet. Give God a chance to speak to you amid your storm.

God always speaks to your storms when they come.

Listen to God's word of encouragement through the Bible.

Go through the following scripture and let God lead the way.

"THEREFORE comfort each other and edify one another, just as you also are doing" 1 Thessalonians 5:11.

"But those who wait on the Lord Shall renew their strength;

They shall mount up with wings like eagles, They shall run and not be weary, They shall walk and not faint" Isaiah 40:31.

"When you pass through the waters, I will be with you; And through the rivers, they shall not overflow you. When you walk through the fire, you shall not be burned, Nor shall the flame scorch you" Isaiah 43:2.

"And the Lord, He is the One who goes before you. He will be with you, He will not leave you nor forsake you; do not fear nor be dismayed" Deuteronomy 31:8.

“Have I not commanded you? Be strong and of good courage; do not be afraid, nor be dismayed, for the Lord your God is with you wherever you go” Joshua 1:9.

“Blessed be the God and Father of our Lord Jesus Christ, the Father of mercies and God of all comfort, who comforts us in all our tribulation, that we may be able to comfort those who are in any trouble, with the comfort with which we ourselves are comforted by God” 2 Corinthians 1:3-4.

“Come to Me, all you who labor and are heavy laden, and I will give you rest” Matthew 11:28.

“I will lift up my eyes to the hills— From whence comes my help? My help comes from the Lord, Who made heaven and earth” Psalm 121:1-2

“Therefore, my beloved brethren, be steadfast, immovable, always abounding in the work of the Lord, knowing that your labor is not in vain in the Lord” 1 Corinthians 15:58

“And let us consider one another in order to stir up love and good works, not forsaking the assembling of ourselves together, as is the manner of some, but exhorting one another, and so much the more as you see the Day approaching” Hebrews 10:24-25

“I will instruct you and teach you in the way you should go; I will guide you with My eye” Psalm 32:8.

“Be of good courage, And He shall strengthen your heart, All you who hope in the Lord" Psalm 31:24.

"Watch, stand fast in the faith, be brave, be strong" 1 Corinthians 16:13.

"These things I have spoken to you, that in Me you may have peace. In the world you will have tribulation; but be of good cheer, I have overcome the world" John 16:33.

"In all labor there is profit, But idle chatter leads only to poverty" Proverbs 14:23.

“Yea, though I walk through the valley of the shadow of death, I will fear no evil; For You are with me; Your rod and Your staff, they comfort me” Psalm 23:4.

“Since you were precious in My sight, You have been honored, And I have loved you; Therefore I will give men for you, And people for your life” Isaiah 43:4.

“Peace I leave with you, My peace I give to you; not as the world gives do I give to you. Let not your heart be troubled, neither let it be afraid” John 14:27.

“For our light affliction, which is but for a moment, is working for us a far more exceeding and eternal weight of glory” 2 Corinthians 4:17.

“What then shall we say to these things? If God is for us, who can be against us? Romans 8:31.

“Now may the God of patience and comfort grant you to be like-minded toward one another, according to Christ Jesus” Romans 15:5.

“And let the beauty of the Lord our God be upon us, And establish the work of our hands for us; Yes, establish the work of our hands” Psalm 90:17.

“Let each of us please his neighbor for his good, leading to edification” Romans 15:2.

“Are not five sparrows sold for two copper coins? And not one of them is forgotten before God. But the very hairs of your head are all numbered. Do not fear therefore; you are of more value than many sparrows” Luke 12:6-7.

“For if there is first a willing mind, it is accepted according to what one has, and not according to what he does not have” 2 Corinthians 8:12

“Therefore we do not lose heart. Even though our outward man is perishing, yet the inward man is being renewed day by day” 2 Corinthians 4:16.

“I, even I, am He who comforts you. Who are you that you should be afraid Of a man who will die, And of the son of a man who will be made like grass?” Isaiah 51:12

“That their hearts may be encouraged, being knit together in love, and attaining to all riches of the full assurance of understanding, to the knowledge of the mystery of God, both of the Father and of Christ” Colossians 2:2.

“They shall neither hunger anymore nor thirst anymore; the sun shall not strike them, nor any heat; for the Lamb who is in the midst of the throne will shepherd them and lead them to living fountains of waters. And God will wipe away every tear from their eyes” Revelation 7:16-17

"For I long to see you, that I may impart to you some spiritual gift, so that you may be established— that is, that I may be encouraged together with you by the mutual faith both of you and me" Romans 1:11-12.

"For as the sufferings of Christ abound in us, so our consolation also abounds through Christ" 2 Corinthians 1:5.

CHAPTER THREE

SANITY IN TIMES OF SUFFERING

The world and suffering are inseparable. You can neither run away nor stop it. God created the earth for humans to live on. Sin altered the original purpose of God, making it difficult to live life to the fullest as God originally planned. But there is good news.

Jesus Christ came to redeem the world from suffering. As a believer, you are free from the fire of suffering and the hopelessness it brings. Thank

God for Jesus and His death on the cross.

Suffering isn't the end of life.

Believers are safe and secure in God's hands.

Nothing can put you out of God's redemption plan.

Do not weep or get depressed when trouble comes.

The comfort of God is always with you.

Sing when you suffer and praise God when you have problems.

"BUT may the God of all grace, who called us to His eternal glory by Christ Jesus, after you have suffered a while, perfect, establish, strengthen, and settle you"1 Peter 5:10.

"Blessed be the God and Father of our Lord Jesus Christ, the Father of mercies and God of all comfort, who comforts us in all our tribulation, that we may be able to comfort those who are in any trouble, with the comfort with which we ourselves are comforted by God" 2 Corinthians 1:3-4.

"And not only that, but we also glory in tribulations, knowing that tribulation produces perseverance; and perseverance, character; and character, hope" Romans 5:3-4.

"For I consider that the sufferings of this present time are not worthy to be compared with the glory which shall be revealed in us" Romans 8:18.

"Many are the afflictions of the righteous, But the Lord delivers him out of them all" Psalm 34:19.

"For our light affliction, which is but for a moment, is working for us a far more exceeding and eternal weight of glory" 2 Corinthians 4:17.

"Who shall separate us from the love of Christ? Shall tribulation, or distress, or persecution, or famine, or nakedness, or peril, or sword?" Romans 8:35.

"Therefore, since Christ suffered for us in the flesh, arm yourselves also with the same mind, for he who has suffered in the flesh has ceased from sin" 1 Peter 4:1.

"But even if you should suffer for righteousness' sake, you are blessed. "And do not be afraid of their threats, nor be troubled" 1 Peter 3:14.

“For to you it has been granted on behalf of Christ, not only to believe in Him, but also to suffer for His sake” Philippians 1:29.

“Bear one another’s burdens, and so fulfill the law of Christ” Galatians 6:2.

“He is despised and rejected by men, A Man of sorrows and acquainted with grief. And we hid, as it were, our faces from Him; He was despised, and we did not esteem Him” Isaiah 53:3.

“Surely He has borne our griefsAnd carried our sorrows; Yet we esteemed Him stricken, Smitten by God, and afflicted” Isaiah 53:4.

“That I may know Him and the power of His resurrection, and the fellowship of His sufferings, being conformed to His death” Philippians 3:10.

“And he who does not take his cross and follow after Me is not worthy of Me” Matthew 10:38.

“For to this you were called, because Christ also suffered for us, leaving us an example, that you should follow His steps" 1 Peter 2:21.

"For as the sufferings of Christ abound in us, so our consolation also abounds through Christ" 2 Corinthians 1:5.

"Then Job arose, tore his robe, and shaved his head; and he fell to the ground and worshiped. And he said: "Naked I came from my mother's womb, And naked shall I return there. The Lord gave, and the Lord has taken away; Blessed be the name of the Lord." Job 1:20-21.

“He who finds his life will lose it, and he who loses his life for My sake will find it” Matthew 10:39.

“So He humbled you, allowed you to hunger, and fed you with manna which you did not know nor did your fathers know, that He might make you know that man shall not live by bread alone; but man lives by every word that proceeds from the mouth of the Lord” Deuteronomy 8:3.

“And though I bestow all my goods to feed the poor, and though I give my body to be burned, but have not love, it profits me nothing" 1 Corinthians 13:3.

"And they stripped Him and put a scarlet robe on Him. When they had twisted a crown of thorns, they put it on His head, and a reed in His right hand. And they bowed the knee before Him and mocked Him, saying, "Hail, King of the Jews!" Matthew 27:28-29

"Behold, happy is the man whom God corrects; Therefore do not despise the chastening of the Almighty" Job 5:17.

“And being in torments in Hades, he lifted up his eyes and saw Abraham afar off, and Lazarus in his bosom. “Then he cried and said, ‘Father Abraham, have mercy on me, and send Lazarus that he may dip the tip of his finger in water and cool my tongue; for I am tormented in this flame.’ ” Luke 16:23-24.

“Therefore, having obtained help from God, to this day I stand, witnessing both to small and great, saying no other things than those which the prophets and Moses said would come— that the Christ would suffer, that He would be the first to rise from the dead, and would proclaim light to the Jewish people and to the Gentiles" Acts 26:22-23.

CHAPTER FOUR

WHOLESOME SPEECH

The words you use on yourself and on other people go a long way to reveal who you truly are. People cannot be deceived for long. Your words give you away as quickly as they come. As a believer, your heart and your mouth must work together to bring glory to God.

God has given you enough Bible verses to guide you on how to use your tongue. Learn them by heart and practice them every day. God uses His word to change our lives. His word molds you into the image of His Son Jesus Christ. God desires you to be like Christ, and this is shown through our actions and words.

Apart from that, the words you use make or break you. Negative words bring negative experiences. Positive words attract positive experiences. Doing neither positive nor negative keeps you on the fence and that is as negative as negative itself. Align your words with God's and watch how good things unfold before your eyes.

Choose your words carefully before you speak.

You are God's mouthpiece for Jesus lives in you.
Use words that please God.

Make the Bible your communication guide.

Repent when you make mistakes with your mouth.

Always ask God for the grace to say the right things.

"DEATH and life are in the power of the tongue, And those who love it will eat its fruit" Proverbs 18:21.

"A good man out of the good treasure of his heart brings forth good; and an evil man out of the evil treasure of his heart brings forth evil. For out of the abundance of the heart his mouth speaks" Luke 6:45.

"Let no corrupt word proceed out of your mouth, but what is good for necessary edification, that it may impart grace to the hearers" Ephesians 4:29.

"He who guards his mouth preserves his life, But he who opens wide his lips shall have destruction" Proverbs 13:3.

"Not returning evil for evil or reviling for reviling, but on the contrary blessing, knowing that you were called to this, that you may inherit a blessing" 1 Peter 3:9.

"A wholesome tongue is a tree of life, But perverseness in it breaks the spirit" Proverbs 15:4.

"Even a fool is counted wise when he holds his peace; When he shuts his lips, he is considered perceptive" Proverbs 17:28.

"But I say to you that for every idle word men may speak, they will give account of it in the day of judgment" Matthew 12:36.

"So then, my beloved brethren, let every man be swift to hear, slow to speak, slow to wrath" James 1:19.

"In the multitude of words sin is not lacking, But he who restrains his lips is wise" Proverbs 10:19.

"Open your mouth for the speechless, In the cause of all who are appointed to die" Proverbs 31:8.

"A man has joy by the answer of his mouth, And a word spoken in due season, how good it is! Proverbs 15:23.

“A soft answer turns away wrath, But a harsh word stirs up anger” Proverbs 15:1.

“My little children, let us not love in word or in tongue, but in deed and in truth” 1 John 3:18.

“For we all stumble in many things. If anyone does not stumble in word, he is a perfect man, able also to bridle the whole body” James 3:2.

“A talebearer reveals secrets, But he who is of a faithful spirit conceals a matter" Proverbs 11:13.

"The words of a wise man's mouth are gracious, But the lips of a fool shall swallow him up" Ecclesiastes 10:12.

"Moreover if your brother sins against you, go and tell him his fault between you and him alone. If he hears you, you have gained your brother" Matthew 18:15.

"Let my mouth be filled with Your praise And with Your glory all the day" Psalm 71:8.

“Therefore whatever you have spoken in the dark will be heard in the light, and what you have spoken in the ear in inner rooms will be proclaimed on the housetops” Luke 12:3.

“That if you confess with your mouth the Lord Jesus and believe in your heart that God has raised Him from the dead, you will be saved” Romans 10:9.

“And when you pray, do not use vain repetitions as the heathen do. For they think that they will be heard for their many words” Matthew 6:7”

“Likewise the Spirit also helps in our weaknesses. For we do not know what we should pray for as we ought, but the Spirit Himself makes intercession for us with groanings which cannot be uttered” Romans 8:26.

“Without counsel, plans go awry, But in the multitude of counselors they are established” Proverbs 15:22.

“Out of the same mouth proceed blessing and cursing. My brethren, these things ought not to be so” James 3:10.

“Oh, give thanks to the Lord! Call upon His name; Make known His deeds among the peoples!” Psalm 105:1.

“Walk in wisdom toward those who are outside, redeeming the time. Let your speech always be with grace, seasoned with salt, that you may know how you ought to answer each one” Colossians 4:5-6.

“So shall My word be that goes forth from My mouth; It shall not return to Me void, But it shall accomplish what I please, And it shall prosper in the thing for which I sent it” Isaiah 55:11.

"Pleasant words are like a honeycomb, Sweetness to the soul and health to the bones" Proverbs 16:24.

"A fool has no delight in understanding, But in expressing his own heart" Proverbs 18:2

"Deliver my soul, O Lord, from lying lips And from a deceitful tongue" Psalm 120:2.

"The hypocrite with his mouth destroys his neighbor, But through knowledge the righteous will be delivered" Proverbs 11:9.

"Let the words of my mouth and the meditation of my heart Be acceptable in Your sight, O Lord, my strength and my Redeemer" Psalm 19:14.

"In all labor there is profit, But idle chatter leads only to poverty" Proverbs 14:23.

"The lips of the righteous know what is acceptable, But the mouth of the wicked what is perverse" Proverbs 10:32.

“Keep your tongue from evil, And your lips from speaking deceit” Psalm 34:13.

“Though I speak with the tongues of men and of angels, but have not love, I have become sounding brass or a clanging cymbal” 1 Corinthians 13:1.

“Anxiety in the heart of man causes depression, But a good word makes it glad” Proverbs 12:25.

“And whatever you do in word or deed, do all in the name of the Lord Jesus, giving thanks to

God the Father through Him" Colossians 3:17.

"A fool's lips enter into contention, And his mouth calls for blows" Proverbs 18:6.

"Whoever hides hatred has lying lips, And whoever spreads slander is a fool" Proverbs 10:18.

"It is honorable for a man to stop striving, Since any fool can start a quarrel" Proverbs 20:3.

"Put away from you a deceitful mouth, And put perverse lips far from you" Proverbs 4:24.

“But above all, my brethren, do not swear, either by heaven or by earth or with any other oath. But let your “Yes” be “Yes,” and your “No,” “No,” lest you fall into judgment” James 5:12.

“But when they arrest you and deliver you up, do not worry beforehand, or premeditate what you will speak. But whatever is given you in that hour, speak that; for it is not you who speak, but the Holy Spirit” Mark 13:11.

“The tongue of the righteous is choice silver; The heart of the wicked is worth little" Proverbs 10:20

"So Jesus answered and said to them, "Assuredly, I say to you, if you have faith and do not doubt, you will not only do what was done to the fig tree, but also if you say to this mountain, 'Be removed and be cast into the sea,' it will be done" Matthew 21:21.

"And have no fellowship with the unfruitful works of darkness, but rather expose them. For it is shameful even to speak of those things which are done by them in secret" Ephesians 5:11-12.

"But as for you, speak the things which are proper for sound doctrine" Titus 2:1.

"For with the heart one believes unto righteousness, and with the mouth confession is made unto salvation" Romans 10:10.

"Blessings are on the head of the righteous, But violence covers the mouth of the wicked" Proverbs 10:6.

"Open your mouth, judge righteously, And plead the

cause of the poor and needy" Proverbs 31:9.

"In my distress I called upon the Lord, And cried out to my God; He heard my voice from His temple, And my cry came before Him, even to His ears" Psalm 18:6.

"When I kept silent, my bones grew old Through my groaning all the day long" Psalm 32:3.

"I will praise You, O Lord, with my whole heart; I will tell of all Your marvelous works" Psalm 9:1.

"By the word of the Lord the heavens were made, And all the host of them by the breath of His mouth" Psalm 33:6.

"Then there appeared to them divided tongues, as of fire, and one sat upon each of them. And they were all filled with the Holy Spirit and began to speak with other tongues, as the Spirit gave them utterance" Acts 2:3-4.

"I will bless the Lord at all times; His praise shall continually be in my mouth" Psalm 34:1.

“For there is not a word on my tongue, But behold, O Lord, You know it altogether” Psalm 139:4.

“I have not departed from the commandment of His lips; I have treasured the words of His mouth More than my necessary food” Job 23:12.

“And I fell to the ground and heard a voice saying to me, ‘Saul, Saul, why are you persecuting Me?” Acts 22:7

“And in that day you will say: “Praise the Lord, call upon His name; Declare His deeds among the peoples, Make mention that His name is exalted" Isaiah 12:4.

"For prophecy never came by the will of man, but holy men of God spoke as they were moved by the Holy Spirit" 2 Peter 1:21.

"Then God said, "Let there be light"; and there was light" Genesis 1:3.

"You are already clean because of the word which I have spoken to you" John 15:3.

"And when they had prayed, the place where they were

assembled together was shaken; and they were all filled with the Holy Spirit, and they spoke the word of God with boldness" Acts 4:31

"Excellent speech is not becoming to a fool, Much less lying lips to a prince" Proverbs 17:7.

"Lying lips are an abomination to the Lord, But those who deal truthfully are His delight" Proverbs 12:22.

"If your brother sins against you, rebuke him; and if he repents, forgive him. And if he sins against you seven times in a day, and seven times in a day returns to you, saying, 'I repent,' you shall forgive him" Luke 17:3b-4.

CHAPTER FIVE

WORD OF GOD IN YOUR HEART AND LIFE

Words of men and women, no matter how wise and helpful, will fail. Good people sometimes make mistakes with their words. They can say nice things now and use swear words later, making a mockery of their human goodness. But God is good and always will. He never says what He doesn't mean or promise what He isn't willing to do.

You need the word of God in these dark times. God is always

there for you. He and His word are one and the same. His words can heal and deliver. It can break the chain of addiction and disperse the cloud of sorrow. God's word in your heart is the remedy for all maladies. Use it each day and don't go a day without a heart filled with the word of God.

God's word isn't ordinary. If humans can use words to motivate others to achieve something, imagine how powerful God's word can be.

God's word is the foundation and raw material for everything that exists and will ever exist.

Storing God's word in the heart and confessing it makes you a powerful believer.

Obeying God’s word transforms your life and makes you Christ-like.

“FOR the word of God is living and powerful, and sharper than any two-edged sword, piercing even to the division of soul and spirit, and of joints and marrow, and is a discerner of the thoughts and intents of the heart” Hebrews 4:12.

“All Scripture is given by inspiration of God, and is profitable for doctrine, for reproof, for correction, for instruction in righteousness, that the man of God may be complete, thoroughly equipped for every good work" 2 Timothy 3:16-17.

"Your word is a lamp to my feet And a light to my path" Psalm 119:105.

"But be doers of the word, and not hearers only, deceiving yourselves" James 1:22.

"How can a young man cleanse his way? By taking heed according to Your word" Psalm 119:9.

"But He said, "More than that, blessed are those who hear the word of God and keep it!" Luke 11:28

"The grass withers, the flower fades, But the word of our God stands forever" Isaiah 40:8.

"As for God, His way is perfect; The word of the Lord is proven; He is a shield to all who trust in Him" Psalm 18:30.

"Therefore whoever hears these sayings of Mine, and does them, I will liken him to a wise man who built his house on the rock" Matthew 7:24.

"Heaven and earth will pass away, but My words will by no means pass away" Matthew 24:35.

"Do all things without complaining and disputing, that you may become blameless and harmless, children of God without fault in the midst of a crooked and perverse generation, among whom you shine as lights in the world, holding fast the word of life" Philippians 2:14-16a.

"The entrance of Your words gives light; It gives

understanding to the simple" Psalm 119:130.

"But He answered and said, "It is written, 'Man shall not live by bread alone, but by every word that proceeds from the mouth of God' "Matthew 4:4.

"In the beginning was the Word, and the Word was with God, and the Word was God" John 1:1God.

"For the word of the Lord is right, And all His work is done in truth" Psalm 33:4.

“He who believes in Me, as the Scripture has said, out of his heart will flow rivers of living water” John 7:38.

“In God (I will praise His word), In God I have put my trust; I will not fear. What can flesh do to me?” Psalm 56:4.

“As newborn babes, desire the pure milk of the word, that you may grow thereby” 1 Peter 2:2.

“For the Lord gives wisdom; From His mouth come knowledge and understanding” Proverbs 2:6.

“Then Jesus said to those Jews who believed Him, “If you abide in My word, you are My disciples indeed. And you shall know the truth, and the truth shall make you free” John 8:31-32.

“Therefore lay aside all filthiness and overflow of wickedness, and receive with meekness the implanted word, which is able to save your souls” James 1:21.

“You have also given me the shield of Your salvation; Your right hand has held me up, Your gentleness has made me great. You enlarged my path under me, So my feet did not slip" Psalm 18:35-36.

"So He humbled you, allowed you to hunger, and fed you with manna which you did not know nor did your fathers know, that He might make you know that man shall not live by bread alone; but man lives by every word that proceeds from the mouth of the Lord" Deuteronomy 8:3.

"And the Word became flesh and dwelt among us, and we beheld His glory, the glory as of the only begotten of the Father, full of grace and truth" John 1:14.

"Who being the brightness of His glory and the express image of His person, and upholding all things by the word of His power, when He had by Himself purged our sins, sat down at the right hand of the Majesty on high" Hebrews 1:3.

"You are my hiding place and my shield; I hope in Your word" Psalm 119:114.

"So shall My word be that goes forth from My mouth; It shall not return to Me void, But it shall accomplish what I please, And it shall prosper in the thing for which I sent it" Isaiah 55:11.

"If you abide in Me, and My words abide in you, you will ask what you desire, and it shall be done for you" John 15:7.

"Every word of God is pure; He is a shield to those who put their trust in Him" Proverbs 30:5.

"My son, give attention to my words; Incline your ear to my sayings. Do not let them depart from your eyes; Keep them in the midst of your heart" Proverbs 4:20-21.

"Let the word of Christ dwell in you richly in all wisdom, teaching and admonishing one another in psalms and hymns and spiritual songs, singing with grace in your hearts to the Lord" Colossians 3:16.

"The entirety of Your word is truth, And every one of Your righteous judgments endures forever" Psalm 119:160.

"Your word I have hidden in my heart, That I might not sin against You" Psalm 119:11.

“I wait for the Lord, my soul waits, And in His word I do hope” Psalm 130:5.

“As for God, His way is perfect; The word of the Lord is proven; He is a shield to all who trust in Him” 2 Samuel 22:31.
“For the Scripture says, “Whoever believes on Him will not be put to shame” Romans 10:11.

“Having been born again, not of corruptible seed but incorruptible, through the word of God which lives and abides forever” 1 Peter 1:23.

“He who calls you is faithful, who also will do it” 1 Thessalonians 5:24.

“The law of the Lord is perfect, converting the soul; The testimony of the Lord is sure, making wise the simple” Psalm 19:7.

“Therefore say to them, ‘Thus says the Lord God: “None of My words will be postponed any more, but the word which I speak will be done,” says the Lord God.’” Ezekiel 12:28.

"Get wisdom! Get understanding! Do not forget, nor turn away from the words of my mouth" Proverbs 4:5.

"Now he who received seed among the thorns is he who hears the word, and the cares of this world and the deceitfulness of riches choke the word, and he becomes unfruitful" Matthew 13:22.

"Hear, my son, and receive my sayings, And the years of your life will be many" Proverbs 4:10"

“You are already clean because of the word which I have spoken to you” John 15:3.

“So he was there with the Lord forty days and forty nights; he neither ate bread nor drank water. And He wrote on the tablets the words of the covenant, the Ten Commandments” Exodus 34:28.

“I have not departed from the commandment of His lips; I have treasured the words of His mouth More than my necessary food” Job 23:12.

“He sent His word and healed them, And delivered them from their destructions” Psalm 107:20.

“This is a faithful saying: For if we died with Him, We shall also live with Him” 2 Timothy 2:11.

“Jesus answered them and said, “My doctrine is not Mine, but His who sent Me” John 7:16.

“All things were made through Him, and without Him nothing was made that was made” John 1:3.

“For assuredly, I say to you, till heaven and earth pass away, one jot or one tittle will by no means pass from the law till all is fulfilled” Matthew 5:18.

“Then those who gladly received his word were baptized; and that day about three thousand souls were added to them” Acts 2:41.

“For I know the thoughts that I think toward you, says the Lord, thoughts of peace and not of evil, to give you a future and a hope” Jeremiah 29:11.

“Why are you cast down, O my soul? And why are you disquieted within me? Hope in God; For I shall yet praise Him, The help of my countenance and my God” Psalm 42:11.

“But those who wait on the Lord Shall renew their strength; They shall mount up with wings like eagles, They shall run and not be weary, They shall walk and not faint” Isaiah 40:31.

“The Lord shall preserve you from all evil; He shall preserve your soul. The Lord shall preserve your going out and your coming in From this time forth, and even forevermore" Psalm 121:7-8.

"Now may the God of hope fill you with all joy and peace in believing, that you may abound in hope by the power of the Holy Spirit" Romans 15:13.

"Now faith is the substance of things hoped for, the evidence of things not seen" Hebrews 11:1.

"Come to Me, all you who labor and are heavy laden, and I will give you rest" Matthew 11:28.

“And now abide faith, hope, love, these three; but the greatest of these is love” 1 Corinthians 13:13.

“And not only that, but we also glory in tribulations, knowing that tribulation produces perseverance; and perseverance, character; and character, hope” Romans 5:3-4.

“You are my hiding place and my shield; I hope in Your word” Psalm 119:114.

“Let us hold fast the confession of our hope without wavering, for He who promised is faithful" Hebrews 10:23.

"Be of good courage, And He shall strengthen your heart, All you who hope in the Lord" Psalm 31:24.

"But if we hope for what we do not see, we eagerly wait for it with perseverance" Romans 8:25.

"Therefore I will look to the Lord; I will wait for the God of my salvation; My God will hear me" Micah 7:7.

“Hope deferred makes the heart sick, But when the desire comes, it is a tree of life” Proverbs 13:12.

““The Lord is my portion,” says my soul, “Therefore I hope in Him!”” Lamentations 3:24.

“Lead me in Your truth and teach me, For You are the God of my salvation; On You I wait all the day” Psalm 25:5.

“I wait for the Lord, my soul waits, And in His word I do hope” Psalm 130:5.

“Let Your mercy, O Lord, be upon us, Just as we hope in You” Psalm 33:22.

“Now hope does not disappoint, because the love of God has been poured out in our hearts by the Holy Spirit who was given to us” Romans 5:5.

“Blessed be the God and Father of our Lord Jesus Christ, who according to His abundant mercy has begotten us again to a living hope through the resurrection of Jesus Christ from the dead” 1 Peter 1:3.

“The Spirit of the Lord God is upon Me, Because the Lord has anointed Me To preach good tidings to the poor; He has sent Me to heal the brokenhearted, To proclaim liberty to the captives, And the opening of the prison to those who are bound” Isaiah 61:1.

“But sanctify the Lord God in your hearts, and always be ready to give a defense to everyone who asks you a reason for the hope that is in you, with meekness and fear” 1 Peter 3:15.

“To them God willed to make known what are the riches of

the glory of this mystery among the Gentiles: which is Christ in you, the hope of glory" Colossians 1:27.

"There is one body and one Spirit, just as you were called in one hope of your calling" Ephesians 4:4.

"So shall the knowledge of wisdom be to your soul; If you have found it, there is a prospect, And your hope will not be cut off" Proverbs 24:14.

"The eyes of your understanding being enlightened; that you may know what is the hope of His calling, what are the riches of the glory of His inheritance in the saints" Ephesians 1:18.

"Does not rejoice in iniquity, but rejoices in the truth; bears all things, believes all things, hopes all things, endures all things" 1 Corinthians 13:6-7.

"The hope of the righteous will be gladness, But the expectation of the wicked will perish" Proverbs 10:28.

CHAPTER SIX

THE HEART OF THE MATTER

Your heart is the heart of all activities going on in your life. You fall or rise based on the condition of your heart. God wants to live in your heart and rule from there. He wants to guide you from within and bring you to your desired destination.

Open your heart to God and let Him in. He will not hurt you; He will heal you. God makes every place he dwells peaceful and perfect. Welcome Him in and hand over the reins of your life.. You will reach your goal even before you know it.

The heart is often the enemy's target. Guard your heart as you would your jewelry.

Once the heart is stolen or taken away, things don't remain the same ever again.

Use God's word to keep your heart and mind intact.

Regular prayers and faith in God's ability to keep you is vital to maintaining a sound heart and mind.

"ABOVE all else, guard your heart, for everything you do flows from it" Proverbs 4:23

“As water reflects the face, so one’s life reflects the heart” Proverbs 27:19.

“The heart is deceitful above all things and beyond cure. Who can understand it? “I the Lord search the heart and examine the mind, to reward each person according to their conduct, according to what their deeds deserve” Jeremiah 17:9-10.

“Your beauty should not come from outward adornment, such as elaborate hairstyles and the wearing of gold jewelry or fine clothes. Rather, it should be that of your inner self, the unfading beauty of a gentle and quiet spirit, which is of great worth in God's sight" 1 Peter 3:3-4.

"You will seek me and find me when you seek me with all your heart" Jeremiah 29:13.

"May he give you the desire of your heart and make all your plans succeed" Psalm 20:4.

"Create in me a pure heart, O God, and renew a steadfast spirit within me" Psalm 51:10.

“But the Lord said to Samuel, “Do not consider his appearance or his height, for I have rejected him. The Lord does not look at the things people look at. People look at the outward appearance, but the Lord looks at the heart” 1 Samuel 16:7.

“Trust in the Lord with all your heart and lean not on your own understanding; in all your ways submit to him, and he will make your paths straight” Proverbs 3:5-6.

“Let love and faithfulness never leave you; bind them around your neck, write them on the tablet of your heart. Then you will win favor and a good name in the sight of God and man" Proverbs 3:3-4.

"Jesus replied: 'Love the Lord your God with all your heart and with all your soul and with all your mind'" Matthew 22:37.

"Take delight in the Lord, and he will give you the desires of your heart" Psalm 37:4.

"For where your treasure is, there your heart will be also" Matthew 6:21.

“A cheerful heart is good medicine, but a crushed spirit dries up the bones” Proverbs 17:22.

“Each of you should give what you have decided in your heart to give, not reluctantly or under compulsion, for God loves a cheerful giver” 2 Corinthians 9:7.

“My son, do not forget my teaching, but keep my commands in your heart, for they will prolong your life many years and bring you peace and prosperity” Proverbs 3:1-2.

“The wise in heart accept commands, but a chattering fool comes to ruin” Proverbs 10:8.

“I will give you a new heart and put a new spirit in you; I will remove from you your heart of stone and give you a heart of flesh” Ezekiel 36:26.

“Be strong and take heart, all you who hope in the Lord” Psalm 31:24.

“I seek you with all my heart; do not let me stray from your commands” Psalm 119:10.

“Teach us to number our days, that we may gain a heart of wisdom” Psalm 90:12.

“May these words of my mouth and this meditation of my heart be pleasing in your sight, Lord, my Rock and my Redeemer” Psalm 19:14.

“Blessed are those who keep his statutes and seek him with all their heart” Psalm 119:2.

“Truly I tell you, if anyone says to this mountain, ‘Go, throw yourself into the sea,’ and does not doubt in their heart but believes that what they say will happen, it will be done for them" Mark 11:23.

"I will praise you with an upright heart as I learn your righteous laws" Psalm 119:7.

But be very careful to keep the commandment and the law that Moses the servant of the Lord gave you: to love the Lord your God, to walk in obedience to him, to keep his commands, to hold fast to him and to serve him with all your heart and with all your soul. Joshua 22:5

“He heals the brokenhearted and binds up their wounds” Psalm 147:3.

“Blessed are the pure in heart, for they will see God” Matthew 5:8”

“Hope deferred makes the heart sick, but a longing fulfilled is a tree of life” Proverbs 13:12.

“Your statutes are my heritage forever; they are the joy of my heart” Psalm 119:111.

“Go, eat your food with gladness, and drink your wine with a joyful heart, for God has already approved what you do" Ecclesiastes 9:7.

"Place me like a seal over your heart, like a seal on your arm; for love is as strong as death, its jealousy unyielding as the grave. It burns like blazing fire, like a mighty flame" Song of Songs 8:6.

"So then, banish anxiety from your heart and cast off the troubles of your body, for youth and vigor are meaningless" Ecclesiastes 11:10.

“Anxiety weighs down the heart, but a kind word cheers it up” Proverbs 12:25.

“And hope does not put us to shame, because God’s love has been poured out into our hearts through the Holy Spirit, who has been given to us” Romans 5:5.

“But I trust in your unfailing love; my heart rejoices in your salvation. I will sing the Lord’s praise, for he has been good to me” Psalm 13:5-6.

“Rend your heart and not your garments. Return to the Lord

your God, for he is gracious and compassionate, slow to anger and abounding in love, and he relents from sending calamity" Joel 2:13.

"I have hidden your word in my heart that I might not sin against you" Psalm 119:11.

"See to it, brothers and sisters, that none of you has a sinful, unbelieving heart that turns away from the living God" Hebrews 3:12.

"My son, pay attention to what I say; turn your ear to my words. Do not let them out of your sight, keep them within your heart" Proverbs 4:20-21.

"Turn my heart toward your statutes and not toward selfish gain" Psalm 119:36.

"My son, if your heart is wise, then my heart will be glad indeed" Proverbs 23:15.

""Even now," declares the Lord, "return to me with all your heart, with fasting and weeping and mourning.'"Joel 2:12.

"I will give thanks to you, Lord, with all my heart; I will tell of all your wonderful deeds" Psalm 9:1.

"Now I am about to go the way of all the earth. You know with all your heart and soul that not one of all the good promises the Lord your God gave you has failed. Every promise has been fulfilled; not one has failed" Joshua 23:14.

"You have heard that it was said, 'You shall not commit adultery.' But I tell you that anyone who looks at a woman lustfully has already committed adultery with her in his heart" Matthew 5:27-28.

“Though an army besiege me, my heart will not fear; though war break out against me, even then I will be confident” Psalm 27:3.

“The precepts of the Lord are right, giving joy to the heart. The commands of the Lord are radiant, giving light to the eyes” Psalm 19:8.

“Teach me your way, Lord, that I may rely on your faithfulness; give me an undivided heart, that I may fear your name” Psalm 86:11.

"Truly he is my rock and my salvation; he is my fortress, I will not be shaken" Psalm 62:6.

CHAPTER SEVEN

STRENGTH FROM HEAVEN

Physical strength has its own place. It helps you go through the physical activities of life. Spiritual strength takes you further than that. It keeps you going when your physical strength fails.

Spiritual strength comes from God and means God's strength in you. When God gives you His strength, imagine the ground you can cover in a lifetime! Recite the scripture below and talk to yourself each day with them and God's life will come on you.

Don't rely on your physical strength as a believer.

Make the word of God your daily source of strength.

Find Bible passages or verses that speak directly to you.

See yourself powerless without the grace and gift of God.

God gives you strength when you depend on Him more.

"FEAR NOT, for I am with you; Be not dismayed, for I am your God. I will strengthen you, Yes, I will help you, I will uphold you with My righteous right hand" Isaiah 41:10.

“But those who wait on the Lord Shall renew their strength; They shall mount up with wings like eagles, They shall run and not be weary, They shall walk and not faint” Isaiah 40:31.

“My flesh and my heart fail; But God is the strength of my heart and my portion forever” Psalm 73:26.

“I can do all things through Christ who strengthens me” Philippians 4:13.

“He gives power to the weak, And to those who have no

might He increases strength" Isaiah 40:29.

"Therefore I take pleasure in infirmities, in reproaches, in needs, in persecutions, in distresses, for Christ's sake. For when I am weak, then I am strong" 2 Corinthians 12:10.

"For God has not given us a spirit of fear, but of power and of love and of a sound mind" 2 Timothy 1:7.

"I will love You, O Lord, my strength. The Lord is my rock and my fortress and my deliverer; My God, my strength, in whom I will trust; My shield and the horn of my salvation, my stronghold" Psalm 18:1-2.

"But the Lord is faithful, who will establish you and guard you from the evil one" 2 Thessalonians 3:3.

"Seek the Lord and His strength; Seek His face evermore!" 1 Chronicles 16:11.

"Watch, stand fast in the faith, be brave, be strong" 1 Corinthians 16:13.

"But I will sing of Your power; Yes, I will sing aloud of Your mercy in the morning; For You have been my defense And refuge in the day of my trouble" Psalm 59:16.

"Ah, Lord God! Behold, You have made the heavens and the earth by Your great power and outstretched arm. There is nothing too hard for You" Jeremiah 32:17.

"The Lord God is my strength; He will make my feet like deer's feet, And He will make me walk on my high hills" Habakkuk 3:19.

“Finally, my brethren, be strong in the Lord and in the power of His might” Ephesians 6:10.

“The Lord is my strength and my shield; My heart trusted in Him, and I am helped; Therefore my heart greatly rejoices, And with my song I will praise Him” Psalm 28:7.

“For the word of God is living and powerful, and sharper than any two-edged sword, piercing even to the division of soul and spirit, and of joints and marrow, and is a discerner of the thoughts and intents of the heart” Hebrews 4:12.

“Now to Him who is able to do exceedingly abundantly above all that we ask or think, according to the power that works in us, to Him be glory in the church by Christ Jesus to all generations, forever and ever. Amen” Ephesians 3:20-21.

“Yours, O Lord, is the greatness, The power and the glory, The victory and the majesty; For all that is in heaven and in earth is Yours; Yours is the kingdom, O Lord, And You are exalted as head over all” 1 Chronicles 29:11.

"'"And you shall love the Lord your God with all your heart, with all your soul, with all your mind, and with all your strength.' This is the first commandment" Mark 12:30.

"So he answered and said to me: "This is the word of the Lord to Zerubbabel: 'Not by might nor by power, but by My Spirit,' Says the Lord of hosts." Zechariah 4:6.

"For the message of the cross is foolishness to those who are perishing, but to us who are being saved it is the power of God. 1 Corinthians 1:18.

“For who is God, except the Lord? And who is a rock, except our God?” Psalm 18:31.

“For they did not gain possession of the land by their own sword, Nor did their own arm save them; But it was Your right hand, Your arm, and the light of Your countenance, Because You favored them” Psalm 44:3.

“For since the creation of the world His invisible attributes are clearly seen, being understood by the things that are made, even His eternal power and Godhead, so that they are without excuse" Romans 1:20.

"For in Him dwells all the fullness of the Godhead bodily; and you are complete in Him, who is the head of all principality and power" Colossians 2:9-10.

"And He said to me, "My grace is sufficient for you, for My strength is made perfect in weakness." Therefore most gladly I will rather boast in my infirmities, that the power of Christ may rest upon me" 2 Corinthians 12:9.

“The Lord will give strength to His people; The Lord will bless His people with peace” Psalm 29:11.
“Though one may be overpowered by another, two can withstand him. And a threefold cord is not quickly broken” Ecclesiastes 4:12.

“Both riches and honor come from You, And You reign over all. In Your hand is power and might; In Your hand it is to make great And to give strength to all” 1 Chronicles 29:12.

"You therefore, my son, be strong in the grace that is in Christ Jesus" 2 Timothy 2:1.

"As for the Almighty, we cannot find Him; He is excellent in power, In judgment and abundant justice; He does not oppress" Job 37:23.

"As His divine power has given to us all things that pertain to life and godliness, through the knowledge of Him who called us by glory and virtue" 2 Peter 1:3.

"'Who has performed and done it, Calling the generations from the beginning? 'I, the Lord, am the first; And with the last I am He'" Isaiah 41:4.

"But you shall receive power when the Holy Spirit has come upon you; and you shall be witnesses to Me in Jerusalem, and in all Judea and Samaria, and to the end of the earth" Acts 1:8.

"For I long to see you, that I may impart to you some spiritual gift, so that you may be established— that is, that I may be encouraged together with you by the mutual faith both of you and me" Romans 1:11-12.

"I will strengthen the house of Judah, And I will save the house of Joseph. I will bring them back, Because I have mercy on them. They shall be as though I had not cast them aside; For I am the Lord their God, And I will hear them" Zechariah 10:6.

"And the angel answered and said to her, "The Holy Spirit will come upon you, and the power of the Highest will overshadow you; therefore, also, that Holy One who is to be born will be called the Son of God"

Luke 1:35.

CHAPTER EIGHT

THOUGHTS ARE THINGS

Your thoughts play an important role in your past, present and future. If you can handle them, you can achieve greater things. Sometimes, you may feel overwhelmed by your past or weighed down by guilt. What you think about your life matters little. So don't beat yourself so hard as though you have ruined your life forever.

What matters is God's word concerning you. If He says He has forgiven you, then accept and get it into your thought life and never look back.

Most times, the reason people find it hard to let go is because they don't see things through God's lenses. Clear your mind of negative thoughts and get God's thoughts into your mind and into your head. His ways are the best you can find in this world and beyond. Don't just try it; do it. It works!

Your thoughts are different from those of God's.

You need to have God's thoughts to receive God's blessings.

God gives you His thoughts through His word.
The Bible has the power to give you God's thoughts.

"SEARCH ME, O God, and know my heart; Try me, and know my anxieties; And see if there is any wicked way in me, And lead me in the way everlasting" Psalm 139:23-24.

"And He said, "What comes out of a man, that defiles a man. For from within, out of the heart of men, proceed evil thoughts, adulteries, fornications, murders, thefts, covetousness, wickedness, deceit, lewdness, an evil eye, blasphemy, pride, foolishness. All these evil things come from within and defile a man"' Mark 7:20-23.

"Commit your works to the Lord, And your thoughts will be established" Proverbs 16:3.

"'For My thoughts are not your thoughts, Nor are your ways My ways," says the Lord" Isaiah 55:8.
"Keep your heart with all diligence, For out of it spring the issues of life" Proverbs 4:23.

"And do not be conformed to this world, but be transformed by the renewing of your mind, that you may prove what is that good and acceptable and perfect will of God" Romans 12:2.

"Finally, brethren, whatever things are true, whatever things are noble, whatever things are just, whatever things are pure, whatever things are lovely, whatever things are of good report, if there is any virtue and if there is anything praiseworthy—meditate on these things" Philippians 4:8.

"O Lord, You have searched me and known me. You know my sitting down and my rising up;

You understand my thought afar off" Psalm 139:1-2.

"Every way of a man is right in his own eyes, But the Lord weighs the hearts" Proverbs 21:2.

"For the word of God is living and powerful, and sharper than any two-edged sword, piercing even to the division of soul and spirit, and of joints and marrow, and is a discerner of the thoughts and intents of the heart" Hebrews 4:12.

"Now I plead with you, brethren, by the name of our

Lord Jesus Christ, that you all speak the same thing, and that there be no divisions among you, but that you be perfectly joined together in the same mind and in the same judgment" 1 Corinthians 1:10.

"Ponder the path of your feet, And let all your ways be established" Proverbs 4:26.

"For what man knows the things of a man except the spirit of the man which is in him? Even so no one knows the things of God except the Spirit of God" 1 Corinthians 2:11.

“Let no one deceive himself. If anyone among you seems to be wise in this age, let him become a fool that he may become wise” 1 Corinthians 3:18.

“I have made a covenant with my eyes; Why then should I look upon a young woman?” Job 31:1.

“There is a way that seems right to a man, But its end is the way of death” Proverbs 14:12.

“And when you pray, do not use vain repetitions as the heathen do. For they think that they will be heard for their many words" Matthew 6:7.

"Therefore gird up the loins of your mind, be sober, and rest your hope fully upon the grace that is to be brought to you at the revelation of Jesus Christ" 1 Peter 1:13.

"Therefore I say to you, do not worry about your life, what you will eat or what you will drink; nor about your body, what you will put on. Is not life more than food and the body more than clothing?" Matthew 6:25.

“Let the wicked forsake his way, And the unrighteous man his thoughts; Let him return to the Lord, And He will have mercy on him; And to our God, For He will abundantly pardon” Isaiah 55:7.

“For I say, through the grace given to me, to everyone who is among you, not to think of himself more highly than he ought to think, but to think soberly, as God has dealt to each one a measure of faith” Romans 12:3.

“Do not worry about your life, what you will eat; nor about the body, what you will put on. Life is more than food, and the body is more than clothing” Luke 12:22b-23.

“Now to Him who is able to do exceedingly abundantly above all that we ask or think, according to the power that works in us, to Him be glory in the church by Christ Jesus to all generations, forever and ever. Amen” Ephesians 3:20-21.

How to Contact the Author

For newly released books, prayers, counseling, daily word and partnership in matters of the kingdom, you can reach George C. Goodman via his Facebook Page and email.

About the Author

George Chukwu Goodman (also known as George Chukwu Ekene) is a powerful voice in the kingdom of God. He is called to preach God's Word in a powerful and life-changing way.

He has served as pastor to several churches and provided spiritual guidance to eight churches all at once. He is a prayer warrior whose prayers have often brought revivals, restoration and miracles to congregations.

Through his writing and discussions, he has provided valuable insights into how best to benefit from the Word of God, how to have Biblical faith, how to develop faith for miracles, signs and wonders, how to meditate on the Word of God, how to have a renewed mind, and many other topics including self-help books that can change lives.

He is a historian, an educator, a poet and a public speaker with a unique and captivating voice. As an author and a multi-talented man, he loves reading good books especially the Bible.

He has tons of books in his personal library where he feeds his soul and renews his mind for more productivity and service.

He is married to Grace George, a godly and praying woman whose support and encouragement cannot be measured by any earthly standard. Together they have two talented, adorable kids. George and Grace live in Lagos, Nigeria.

Books by the Same Author

Prayer and Unshakable Faith

Heal Your Life with God's Promises Book 3

Heal Your Life with God's Promises Book 2

Heal Your Life with God's Promises Book 1

Heal Your Marriage God's Way

New Life in God's Promises

A Dozen Grace Instant Devotional

Practical Questions That Are Not Supposed to be Left Unanswered

Prayers that Expose Secret Enemies and Open New Doors

Holy Spirit's Power ESV

Holy Spirit's Power NKJV

30 Days in the School of Faith

(FREE)

Bigger Better Bolder (FREE)

The Throne of Grace

How to FREE the CHRIST in

You

Prayer and Unshakable Faith

www.ingramcontent.com/pod-product-compliance
Ingram Content Group UK Ltd.
Pitfield, Milton Keynes, MK11 3LW, UK
UKHW021936190726
13853UKWH00004B/1477

9 798523 840944